A "Beastly" Christmas

A Comedy For All Ages

John O. Eby

Illustrations by
Natividad Briones

CSS Publishing Company, Inc., Lima, Ohio

A "BEASTLY" CHRISTMAS

Scripture quotations are from the New Revised Standard Version of the Bible, copyright
1989 by the Division of Christian Education of the National Council of the Churches of
Christ in the USA. Used by permission.

For more information about CSS Publishing Company resources, visit our website at
www.csspub.com or email us at custserv@csspub.com or call (800) 241-4056.

Companion coloring books (0-7880-2384-5) are available in packages of five(s), from
the above sites.

Cover design by Nikki Nocera
ISBN 978-0-7880-2382-8   PRINTED IN U.S.A.

I would like to dedicate this drama
to Enoch H. Eby, my grandfather and spiritual mentor
and to Sherrie Eby, my wife and spiritual partner

Acknowledgments

I would like to acknowledge my Lord and Savior, Jesus Christ, for the inspiration he gives to the dramas I have written.

I would also like to acknowledge Tami Hensley, my dedicated secretary, and Carolynn Magowan, who has directed over twenty of the dramas and skits I have written.

Table Of Contents

Introduction

This drama was first presented at First Baptist Church of Porterville, California, in 1997, and presented again in 2004. It has been one of the most warmly received programs of all that we have done.

It is presented in a unique fashion. The voices of the animals were performed offstage by a group of adults. The human characters (nonspeaking) were performed by children — camel masters, angels, shepherds, Mary, and Joseph.

The characterizations, drawn by Natividad Briones, may be flashed on a screen by using an overhead projector or by PowerPoint© presentation, available to purchasers at http://www.csspub.com/BeastlyChristmas/.

With the adult choir and the youth/children's choir leading the musical segments, this involves many members of the congregation, but requires very few rehearsals.

Our church has an average attendance of 100, so a large congregation is not required. Our choir was actually an octet, and some of them were animal voices, as well. Some of the children's choir members were also in the nativity. Larger churches could make this much more elaborate, but it was both effective and fun with a smaller cast.

You could choose to use costuming and not use the picture presentation for a more traditional program.

May God bless you,
John and Sherrie Eby

Production Notes

Characters

Speaking
Caleb, Casbah, and Cashmere Camel
Daniel Donkey
Katrina, Bessie, and Morticia Cow
Shilo, Shelby, and Sherlock Sheep

Nonspeaking
Camel masters (three)
Angels (four or more)
Shepherds (three or more)
Mary, Joseph

Setting
These suggestions are based on our presentation of this program, but it is very flexible and easily adaptable.

We put the screen stage left with the animal readers seated below. The nativity scene was center stage and the adult choir stage right.

The children's choir was seated in the front rows of the congregation and they moved in front of the nativity, center stage, when they sang.

Costumes
Camel Masters — robes
Angels — white robes and halos
Shepherds — robes
Mary and Joseph — robes

Props
Overhead projector or PowerPoint© program
Screen
Manger and baby doll
Straw bales for Mary and Joseph
Shiny star above the manger

Posters
Poster samples for you to copy are on pages 10-11. Replace the information with your church's name, address, date, and presentation time.

This will help you advertise your upcoming program with your church's individual flavor.

A Christmas Comedy

First Baptist Church
Christmas Program

Something *exciting* is happening!

What? Where? When?

Christmas Comedy

First Baptist Church

101 North G Street, Porterville

December 14, 1997 - 11:00 A.M.

I hope *I* don't forget!

DON'T FORGET!

December 14th

11:00 A.M.

First Baptist Church

Music

This humorous presentation is tied together with songs. The adult choir sings five songs during the presentation and the children's choir sings parts of "The Friendly Beasts" song throughout the presentation, as well.

This is a Medieval Christmas Chant (Orientis Partibus 2, 77.77 — in the public domain) commonly called "The Friendly Beasts" to which we have added a verse for our presentation.

Adult choir songs include "O Sing A Song Of Bethlehem" (words by Louis Benton, traditional hymn tune "O I Feel The Winds Of God Today") or "O Little Town Of Bethlehem," "Away In A Manger," "Angels We Have Heard On High," "Shepherds Shake Off Your Drowsy Sleep" or "While Shepherds Watched Their Flocks By Night," and "Christmas Joy Medley" by Tom Fettke (copyright 1986 Pilot Point Music).

The congregation joins the choirs in singing "Joy To The World," which is the closing hymn.

Christmas Medieval Chant
Music: John Eby
Words: Medieval English Carol
Camel verse by John Eby

Jesus, our Brother, kind and good
Was humbly born in a stable rude,
And friendly beasts around him stood;
Jesus, our Brother, kind and good.

Thus said the camel, sturdy and strong,
"Loaded with gifts we traveled along
But in my heart I carried a song."
Thus said the camel, sturdy and strong.

Thus said the donkey, shaggy and brown,
"I carried his mother up hill and down;
I carried his mother to Bethlehem town."
Thus said the donkey, shaggy and brown.

Thus said the cow, all white and red,
"I gave him my manger for a bed,
I gave him my hay to cradle his head."
Thus said the cow, all white and red.

Thus said the sheep with the curly horn,
"I gave him my wool for his blanket warm.
He wore my coat on Christmas morn."
Thus said the sheep with the curly horn.

Thus every beast by some good spell
In the stable was glad to tell
Of the gift he gave to Emmanuel,
The gift he gave Emmanuel.

Orientis Partibus 2, 77.77

Medieval French melody

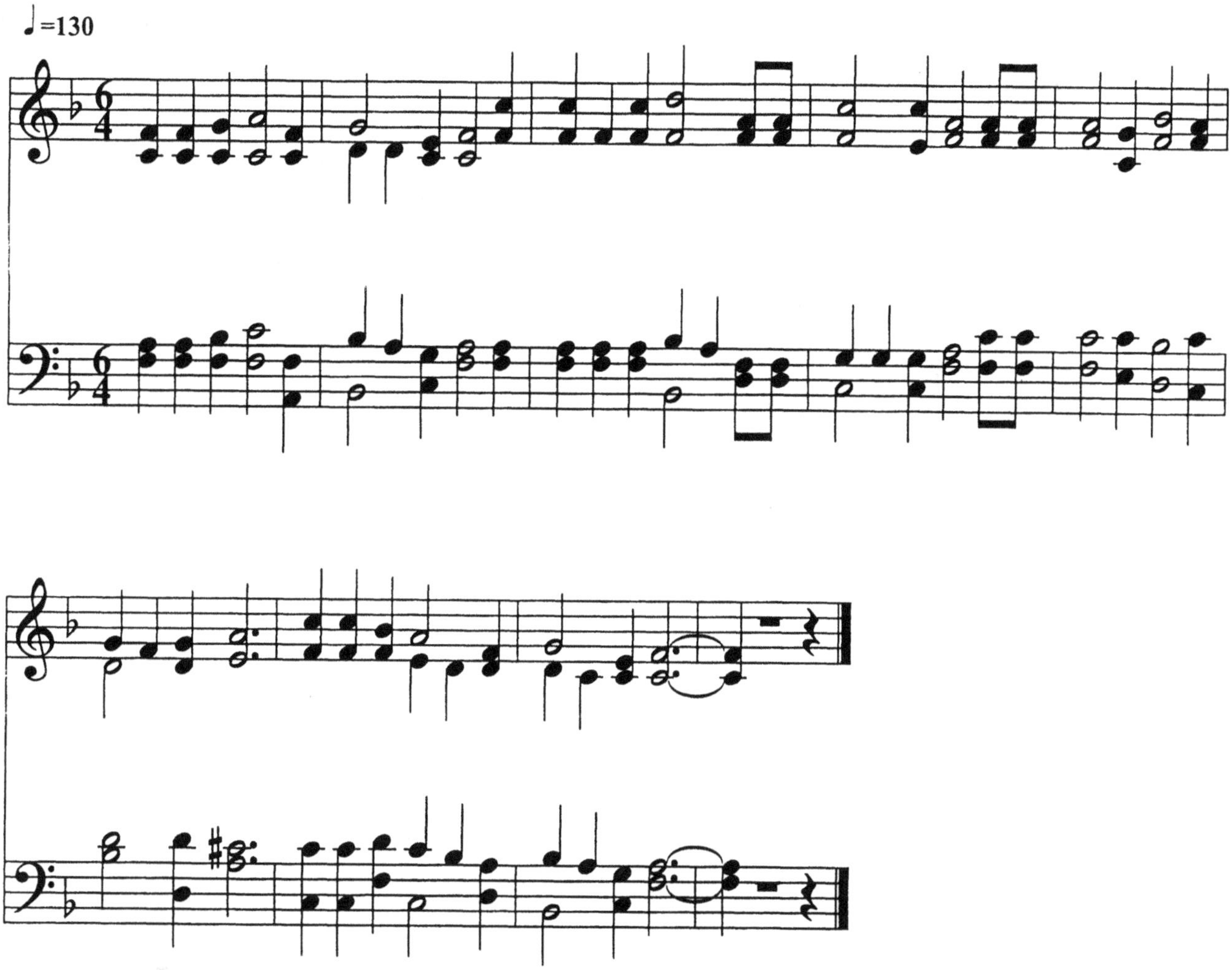

Program And Script

(Pastor calls children forward)

Could all of the children please come forward? *(give them time to come up and gather around you)*

Hello, boys and girls. Do you know what is going to happen here this evening? *(let them answer)* That is correct, we are going to have a special program. This program will tell us the story of Jesus' birth through the eyes of the animals who were there. Did you ever wonder what animals might be thinking? *(let them answer)* I do. I wonder what makes dogs bark or cats meow. I wonder what cows are saying when they moo to each other.

Tonight we are going to watch and listen as camels, sheep, cows, and a donkey tell us a very special story. These are modern animals, so they may have jewelry or a mustache, and they like to make us laugh. I want to introduce you to the characters in our program: **to CS1**

Caleb Camel	**to CS2**
Casbah Camel	**to CS3**
Cashmere Camel	**to CS4**
Daniel Donkey	**to CS5**
Katrina Cow	**to CS6**
Morticia Cow	**to CS7**
Bessie Cow	**to CS8**
Shilo Sheep	**to CS9**
Shelby Sheep	
and last, but not least,	**to CS10**
Sherlock Sheep	**to Cover**

We will have coloring books for you to take home to help remind you of the story you will hear tonight. Please bring them back and share with us your beautiful work.

I am going to ask you to return to your seats now and get ready for this very special presentation, and I want to thank you for bringing your friends and family with you this evening.

(Allow time for all to return and settle in their seats and then adjust the lighting and begin the production.)

Adult Reader

Christmas comes to many lands, but none so grand as here.
Here amongst the animals, angels cause no fear.
For we among the wildlife know that God is king.
We are his creation, every living thing. **to SN1**

(Children's choir sings first verse and camel verse of "The Friendly Beasts.")

Jesus, our Brother, kind and good
Was humbly born in a stable rude,
And friendly beasts around him stood;
Jesus, our Brother, kind and good.

Thus said the camel, sturdy and strong,
"Loaded with gifts we traveled along
But in my heart I carried a song."
Thus said the camel, sturdy and strong.

to CP1

Caleb: What are you doing out in the middle of the night?

to CP2

Casbah: I could ask you the same thing!

to CP3

Cashmere: Hello, my dramatic friends!

to CP4

Caleb: What is so dramatic about us?

to CP5

Cashmere: Thought you would never ask. We are "drama-deries" aren't we?

to CP6

Casbah: O brother! Can we get serious? What are you doing here, Cashmere?

to CP7

Cashmere: I was awakened by a star, and I don't mean Brad Pitt! I mean a star in the sky, bright enough to awaken a horse — or camel!

to CP8

Casbah: You saw it, too? It's still up there shining like blazes. My master saddled me and rode me over here to your master's house, Caleb, so that he could talk to your master about it.

to CP9

Cashmere: Your master, Caleb, your master Casbah, and my master all together? Trying to figure something out? Sounds like they are trying to "master mind" a great plot!

to CP10

Caleb: This star is a real sign from God! Something great is about to happen! And I suspect that we shall be a part of it.

to CP11

(Camel masters enter and stand center stage, pretending to talk with each other.)

Casbah: Look, our three masters have come outside and are talking rather excitedly. They are looking at the star. Caleb, you have the best ears. Can you make out what they are saying?

to CP12

Caleb: Hmm ... something about the birth of a king of the ... ahh, the Jews. Okay ... sounds like we are all going to be leaving in the morning.

to CP13

(Camel masters slowly leave the stage area and return to their seats.)

to CP14

Casbah: They're breaking up!

to CP15

Cashmere: Wow! I didn't know they were even engaged!

to SN1

Casbah: Here they come! Guess we're headed for one great adventure!

(Adult choir sings "O Sing A Song of Bethlehem" or "O Little Town Of Bethlehem.")

(Children's choir sings the donkey verse of "The Friendly Beasts.")
Thus said the donkey, shaggy and brown,
"I carried his mother up hill and down;
I carried his mother to Bethlehem town."
Thus said the donkey, shaggy and brown.

to CP16

Daniel: What a happy task was mine! I got to carry Mary on my back for six days as we came here from Nazareth. It was a long, hard trip, up steep trails, down into rich, fertile valleys, and then back up to the rugged ridges. Joseph pushed us as hard as he could because they did not want to travel on the Sabbath, but we had to travel at a pace that Mary could handle. I tried to walk as gently as I could, for I knew I was carrying a miracle!

We got to Bethlehem almost at sundown. Many of Mary and Joseph's relatives had started out with us, but because we had to come at a slower pace, they arrived first. Joseph stopped us at a couple of places and then, just minutes before sundown, a man gave us permission to stay in his barn. I was right at home and it did not take Joseph long to make a comfortable nest in the straw for Mary.

to SN1

(Mary and Joseph take their places in the nativity scene. Baby doll is hidden from the view of the audience.)

(Adult choir sings "Away In A Manger.")

(Children's choir sings the cattle verse of "The Friendly Beasts.")
    Thus said the cow, all white and red,
    "I gave him my manger for a bed,
    I gave him my hay to cradle his head."
    Thus said the cow, all white and red.

to CP17

to CP18

Katrina: Say, Bessie, what is happening in that stall next to you?

Bessie: You would never believe it, Katrina! This woman over here is giving birth! Oh, I understand her pain, but I know the thrill of bringing a little one into the world! What can you see, Morticia? *(Mary carefully places doll in manger.)* **to CP19**

Morticia: Awww! What a cute little one, I mean for a human. I guess *any* baby will warm your heart, but somehow this one is special! **to CP20**

Bessie: Yes, since these humans arrived I have felt that God has anointed this day in a unique way. **to CP21**

Katrina: Well, whatever they do, I hope they won't make too much noise. I must get my beauty sleep! **to CP22**

Morticia: Sleep, schleep! I have a feeling that we're not going to get much of that tonight. I am so excited, I can hardly hold my milk in! **to CP23**

Bessie: *(laughing)* Morticia, you are so excitable! But you know, Katrina, I have to agree with Morticia. I think we have just begun to experience some exciting things. I think you can forget sleep tonight! **to CP24**

Katrina: O bother! I can see a bad day coming! No sleep, so I will have bags under my eyes tomorrow. No hope of impressing that handsome bull in the next field! On top of that, Farmer Jacob will probably have cold hands. **to CP25**

Bessie: Katrina, try to look on the bright side. We are witnessing a miracle here!

to SN1

(Children's choir sings the sheep verse of "The Friendly Beasts.")
  Thus said the sheep with the curly horn,
  "I gave him my wool for his blanket warm.
  He wore my coat on Christmas morn."
  Thus said the sheep with the curly horn.

(Shepherds approach center stage and face audience, unaware of nativity scene behind them.)

to CP26

Shilo: Stand baaaaaack, all you commoners! Shilo, the great, is here to watch over you!

to CP27

Shelby: Yes, "your highness," it is good that you are here! We probably didn't need these helpless, human shepherds around with the "mighty Shilo" here.

to CP28

Shilo: Stuff your mouth with jimsonweed, Shelby, and may the briars get stuck in your wool! You know these frail humans are only here because we let them think they are in charge.

to CP29

Sherlock: Say, you two "bleating heart wool-bearers," could you move your debate to another field so I can get some sleep? I have a feeling that God is going to do something unique tonight and we are going to need our rest.

to CP30

Shilo: I'm sorry, Sherlock! I feel a little "sheepish." It was baaaad manners to be making so much noise. Shelby and I get a little carried away with our teasing sometimes.

to CP31

Shelby: Speak for yourself! It is a sheer delight "pulling the wool" over your eyes. I'm serious!

to CP32

Shilo: You're serious? Well, I'm *Roebuck*. Who is watching the store?

to CP33

Sherlock: *(laughing)* Enough, enough all ready!

(One Angel enters and stands center stage in front of nativity scene.)   **to CP34**

Shilo: Hey! Yo! Who is that talking to the shepherds?   **to CP35**

Shelby: Why, it's an angel! What is she saying?   **to CP36**

Sherlock: She's saying, "Don't be afraid, for I bring good news which is meant for everyone. For this very night, in Bethlehem, a baby is born who is the Savior, Christ the Lord!"   **to CP37**

Shilo: Afraid? Who would be afraid of an angel?

(More Angels enter and stand near first Angel, in a cluster, facing audience.)   **to CP38**

Shelby: *They* are! Look at them. They look like a bunch of scared sheep! Pardon the pun.   **to CP39**

Shilo: Ho! What! There must be a zillion angels. Listen to them sing!   **to SN1**

(Adult choir sings "Angels We Have Heard On High.")   **to CP40**

Sherlock: I told you! I knew something special was going to happen tonight! I knew it! I knew it!   **to CP41**

Shilo: Where did you get your clue, Sherlock, from the "clues closet"?

(Shepherds move to the front and stand together on the readers' side of the Angel cluster.)   **to CP42**

Shelby: Whew, here come the shepherds. They look like they are going somewhere.   **to CP43**

Shilo: Yeah, my guess is that they are headed for Bethlehem.   **to CP44**

Sherlock: I want to go, too! I want to see this great thing God has done! Let's let them know we want to go, also!

to CP45

Shilo, Shelby, and Sherlock: *("bleat" and "baa" vigorously)*

to SN1

(Adult choir sings "Shepherds Shake Off Your Drowsy Sleep" or "While Shepherds Watch Their Flocks By Night.")

(Shepherds leave the area during the song and return to their seats.)

to CP46

Shelby: *(whispering)* You were right, Sherlock! There is something wonderful happening here. There is such a sense of God's delight at what is taking place.

to CP47

Sherlock: This is breathtaking! These cows have been here all along. Let's ask them what happened.

to CP48

Katrina: First a baby was born ... now a herd of sheep! This place is becoming a real zoo! What is a lady to do?

to CP49

Bessie: Welcome, our wooly friends! What brings you to our abode at such an hour?

to CP50

Sherlock: Well, it has been some night! We were resting in the hills just outside of town and Angels came and told our masters ...

to CP51

Shilo: He means our servants ...

to CP52

Sherlock: ... that a child would be born who would be a Savior, a Deliverer, Lord to all people all over the world. So we begged our masters ...

to CP53

Shilo: ... our servants ...

to CP54

Sherlock: ... to let us come along. What has happened here?

to CP55

21

Bessie: It has been quite a night here, too! God is definitely doing something dynamic here tonight!

to CP56

Katrina: God, or whoever, is ruining a good night's sleep, that is what he is doing!!Seems like all this *could* have been planned for daytime!

to CP57

Morticia: Peek through the slats in the stall! You can see him! A little baby was born here tonight ... right here in this stable. Just about sundown they came ... the woman was riding on Daniel over there ... then they got settled in and that beautiful baby was born.

to CP58

Daniel: Mary started to feel the pains of birth within an hour after we settled down. In the middle of the night I heard the crying of a new baby ... and I knew the waiting was over. God was at work, and I knew it! What a privilege it was to be a small part of bringing God's will into being.

You say that the angel said that this baby is destined to be the Savior, the Deliverer, the Lord? I knew I was carrying a miracle, but ... wow ... I had no idea!

(Camel masters enter and stand with Shepherds.)

to CP59

Katrina: Hey! Ho! What's this? This is no zoo, *it's a three-ring circus!*

to CP60

Caleb: Pardon the disturbance. May we come in?

to CP61

Katrina: Yeah, well come on in. Might as well join the party!

to CP62

Bessie: Welcome, dear friends! What brings you here?

to CP63

Cashmere: We were following Brad Pitt ... no, no, just joking. We were following a very bright star and it seemed to stop right over this stable.

to CP64

Bessie: Angels ... a bright star ... something *very dramatic* is happening here tonight!

to CP65

Casbah: Don't say "dramatic" ...

to CP66

Cashmere: That's why we're here! We make things dramatic! After all, we are "drama-deries"!

to CP67

Casbah: Too late ... 1,000 miles of corny jokes ... we are the only "corn fed" camels on the planet.

to CP68

Sherlock: *(laughing)* I see you have a jokester, too. I suggest we lock Cashmere and Shilo in a stall together and let them tell corny jokes to each other until one or the other gets "joked to death"!

to CP69

Everyone: *(laughs)*

to CP70

Bessie: Seriously, though, do you realize that we are firsthand witnesses to the greatest event in history? God has come into the world in human form, in this little baby!

to CP71

Sherlock: And what a privilege it is to be here. Our masters were chosen to hear the good news first, so we are all witnesses to the greatest miracle the world has ever known.

to CP72

Caleb: And the amazing thing is that out there most people don't even realize what a miracle this is, and what this miracle means for them.

to CP73

Katrina: Keep talking! I am beginning to think this *might* be worth giving up a night's sleep.

to CP74

Bessie: See, I *told* you, miracles are happening!

to CP75

Cashmere: Can I say a word?

to CP76

Everyone: NO! *(begin to laugh)*

to CP77

Morticia: I am just so excited! I just want to sing and shout and praise God!

to CP78

(Music for "The Friendly Beasts" should begin playing very softly in the background as Bessie speaks.)

Bessie: That is exactly what we ought to do ... "Praise the Lord from the Earth, you great sea creatures and all ocean depths, lightning and hail, snow and clouds, stormy winds that do his bidding, you mountains and all hills, fruit trees and all cedars, wild animals and all cattle, small creatures and flying birds, kings of the Earth and all nations, you princes and all rulers on the Earth, young men and maidens, old men and children. Let everything that has breath, praise the Lord." *Praise the Lord!*

(Children's choir sings the last verse of "The Friendly Beasts.")
    Thus every beast by some good spell
    In the stable was glad to tell
    Of the gift he gave to Emmanuel,
    The gift he gave Emmanuel.

(Shepherds, Masters, and Angels pay homage to the Baby Jesus by bowing before him.)

(Adult choir sings "Christmas Joy Medley" during the bowing.)

(Congregation joins the adult choir and children's choir in the singing of the closing hymn, "Joy To The World.")

Slide Guide
With Printout

A "Beastly" Christmas

Cover

CS1

CS2

CS3

CS4

CS5

CS6

CS7

CS8

CS9

CS10

A "Beastly" Christmas

Cover

SN1

CP1

CP2

CP3

CP4

CP5

CP6

CP7

CP8

CP9

CP10

CP11

CP12

CP13

CP14

CP15

SN1

CP16

SN1

CP17

CP18

CP19

CP20

CP21

CP22

CP23

CP24

CP25

SN1

CP26

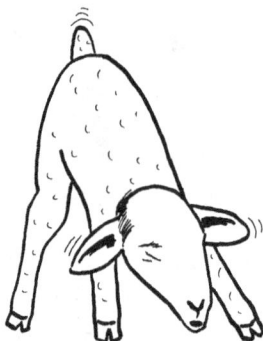

CP27

CP28

CP29

CP30

CP31

CP32

CP33

CP34

CP35

CP36

CP37

CP38

CP39

SN1

CP40

CP41

CP42

CP43

31

CP44

CP45

SN1

CP46

CP47

CP48

CP49

CP50

CP51

CP52

CP53

CP54

CP55

CP56

CP57

CP58

CP59

CP60

CP61

CP62

CP63

CP64

CP65

CP66

CP67

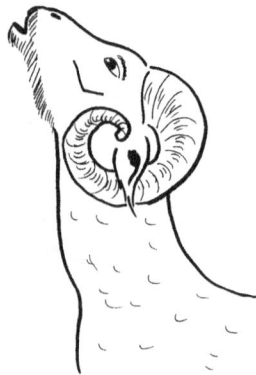

CP68

CP69

CP70

CP71

CP72

CP73

CP74

CP75

CP76

CP77

CP78

Notes

www.ingramcontent.com/pod-product-compliance
Lightning Source LLC
Chambersburg PA
CBHW081549040426
42448CB00015B/3267